T0011989

Football Isn't
Football?

Arturo Castillón
Jimmy Moorhead

VISTA®
HIGHER LEARNING

Boston, Massachusetts

ELA

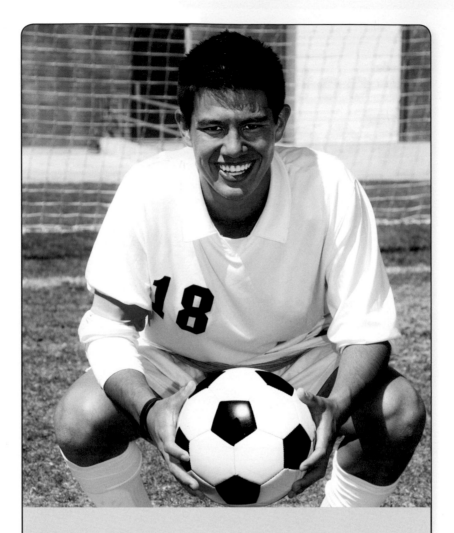

Name: Luis Montego

Age: 15

From: Guatemala City

Favorite sport: Too many to count!

Favorite team: Comunicaciones F.C.

Likes: playing sports, playing the guitar, eating

Dislikes: sleeping, singing

This is Luis, a student from Guatemala City, Guatemala. He's 15 years old and he really loves sports—especially soccer! Luis plays sports every day and even plays on his school team. His team usually wins, and that makes Luis happy. Sometimes they lose, though, and Luis doesn't like that at all. He loves sports and he *really* loves winning!

Luis has a good friend named Mary. She's an American from Los Angeles, California. She goes to a local high school and is very interested in Latin American studies.

She has studied Spanish for several years and really enjoys it. In fact, she and Luis met in Guatemala two years ago when she was studying Spanish in Guatemala City. They became very close friends at the time and have kept in touch ever since.

They often write and e-mail to talk about what's happening in their lives. Then, one day Mary decided to send Luis a special update and invitation!

Luis and Mary kept in touch. They wrote letters and e-mails and talked on the phone.

Hi Luis,

How are things? Life here in L.A. is great! I started going to my new school last week. It's really fun! There are a lot of fun activities to take part in, and I'm having a good time. (Check out this activity announcement!)

Last week we had a Latin American party in my Spanish class. It was great, but speaking Spanish made me miss you and all my friends there! Please come for a visit. My family would love to see you and there are so many interesting things to do in L.A. You would have a great time! Please talk to your parents and see what they say. Maybe they can bring you?

Write soon!

Mary

SOUTH POINT HIGH SCHOOL ACTIVITIES

Sports	Music	Clubs
basketball	choir	drama
tennis	band	chess
baseball	dance	robotics
soccer		gaming
football		math
hockey		science

As soon as Luis read the e-mail, he knew he would love to go and visit his friend. He showed the e-mail to his mother and asked if there was a chance they could go. His mom and dad had a long talk about it and decided that it would be a good chance for Luis to see his friend, and for him to learn a bit more about American culture. Off to Los Angeles it would be!

Luis and his mother arrived in California a month later and went directly to Mary's house. Mary and Luis were really happy to see each other. They started making plans to do as many activities as possible while Luis was there. Luis was looking forward to learning more about the United States and having some fun!

"What do you want to do, first?" asked Mary.

"I don't know," replied Luis. "Do you have any ideas?

"Yes, I do!" answered Mary. "Let's go to a football game! There's a game at my school today. It's a really popular sport here, and it would be a great way for you to get to know the game," she said excitedly.

"That sounds great!" Luis answered quickly. "I'm not sure how many *new* things I'll learn. I love football, but maybe I can learn *something*!"

"Excellent," replied Mary. "It starts at 2:00. Let's go!"

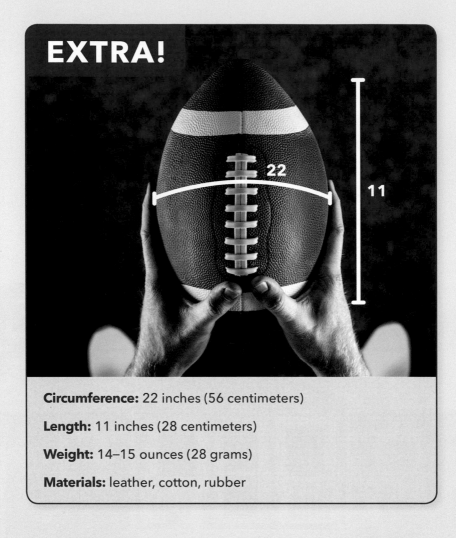

EXTRA!

22

11

Circumference: 22 inches (56 centimeters)

Length: 11 inches (28 centimeters)

Weight: 14–15 ounces (28 grams)

Materials: leather, cotton, rubber

Mary's mom drove her and Luis to the football **stadium**. As she went to park the car, they went into the game to find some seats. Then, they sat down and took a look at the **field**.

As Luis looked around, he started watching the teams out on the field warming up. They were playing with a ball and throwing it around. But their ball was brown, not black and white like his football. It looked very different!

football field

uniform

helmet

Then, Luis looked at the **players**. They looked really different, too. They were wearing helmets and strange **uniforms**. They weren't wearing T-shirts and shorts likes Luis's team. He didn't get it, so he decided to say something to Mary. "Mary," he began. "This game is absolutely *not* football!"

Mary gave Luis a strange look. "Yes, it is!" she replied. "What are you talking about?"

Luis quickly took out his phone and showed Mary a photo of a black and white ball. Luis pointed to the ball and said with **confidence**, "*This* is a football." Then, he pointed to the field and added, "That game is *not* football!"

Mary looked at him strangely, and then she began to laugh softly. "Oh," Mary began slowly. "Now I understand." She pointed to Luis's phone. "This is *not* a football," she said. "This is a *soccer* ball!"

"What? My football isn't a football?" Luis asked in **confusion**. "What are you saying?"

Mary laughed again. "We're in the United States," she explained with a smile. She pointed to Luis's picture. "This is called a soccer ball here." Then, Mary pointed out on the field to one of the brown balls. "*That* is called a football here. And this game is called football here. It's *American football*," she explained.

Luis and Mary looked at each other and started laughing. They finally understood what was going on. People call the game soccer "football" in Guatemala. But in the United States, "football" is a completely different game. It was a really funny mistake for both of them!

"OK, so now that we understand each other a little
better, teach me about American football, Mary!"
said Luis with excitement.

"Sure," replied Mary with a smile. "There are a lot of
rules that are different from the game you know, but
I can teach you some important things."

Mary and Luis looked out at the field. The players were lining up on two sides of a line in the center of the field. After a few minutes, the game began. One player threw the ball between his knees, and another player behind him caught it. That player threw the ball down the field. It flew through the air, and a third player caught it by jumping and grabbing it quickly with his hands. He carried the ball down the field, running fast and keeping the ball safe against his stomach.

All of this was a big surprise for Luis. "Wait a minute!" he said in surprise. "You can't use your hands! It's against the rules!"

Mary smiled. "You have to remember that this isn't soccer, Luis. It's American football, and you can catch and throw with your hands as much as you want," she explained.

KNOW IT ALL

In American football, players can use their hands and feet. They must carry, throw, or kick the ball across a special line called the goal line.

offensive player

defensive player

Mary and Luis watched the game for a while more. Luis thought it was strange. Some players just stood there, and then suddenly they'd start pushing and pulling other players down. Mary pointed to those players. "Those are the **defensive** players," she said. "They want to stop the ball from going down the field."

Luis watched some more. Other players ran, jumped, and moved quickly to get the ball and carry it down the field. Mary pointed to those players. "Those are the **offensive** players," she explained. "Their job is to carry the ball down the field and try to get it across that white line."

"I see," replied Luis thoughtfully. It was all very interesting —but different! "It kind of looks like those offensive players are dancing!" Luis joked. Mary agreed with a laugh as they continued watching the game.

14

EXTRA!

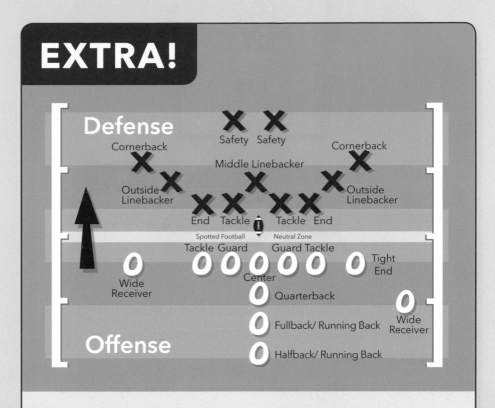

Defense

Cornerback

Safety   Safety

Cornerback

Middle Linebacker

Outside
Linebacker

Outside
Linebacker

End   Tackle   Tackle   End

Spotted Football   Neutral Zone

Tackle Guard   Guard Tackle

Tight
End

Wide
Receiver

Center

Quarterback

Wide
Receiver

Offense

Fullback/ Running Back

Halfback/ Running Back

OFFENSIVE AND DEFENSIVE TEAMS IN AMERICAN FOOTBALL

In American football, the offensive team moves the ball down the field. They can kick, carry, or pass (meaning throw) the ball.

The defensive team tries to stop the offensive team. They can tackle (meaning pull down) the offensive players. They can also catch the ball. This is called an interception.

fly

Luis looked around the field again and noticed two huge poles at each end of the field. "What are those?" he asked in surprise. "They're really tall!"

Mary explained they were for scoring. Luis's eyes grew big as he asked, "And how do players get up there to make a goal? Do they fly?"

That made Mary laugh again, as she explained how to score in football. She told Luis that the two poles were called **goal posts**. She then explained that players needed to run the ball over the white **line** near the goal posts to score what's called a **touchdown**. She added that another option for scoring was to kick the ball between the two poles to score an extra point or a field goal. "I see," replied Luis. "Well, that makes a lot more sense than flying!"

EXTRA!

Football Goal Posts

Width: 18 feet 6 inches (5.64 meters)

Height: 20 feet at poles (6.1 meters)
10 feet at crossbar (3 meters)

Materials: wood, paint, cement

goal post

crossbar

pole

goal line

touchdown

The two friends laughed and shared a smile, but they quickly turned back to the game as the crowd went wild. A defensive player had gotten the ball. It was an interception! He was running really fast, and it looked like the offensive team wouldn't be able to stop him. He did it! He carried the ball over the goal line and scored a touchdown for the red team! Mary and Luis both stood up to cheer. Mary's school team had made a point! There wasn't much time left in the game, and this was going to give her school a good chance at winning!

A few moments later, the red team lined up and kicked the ball. It went through the goal posts. "Yes!" shouted Mary. "That's seven points for my team!"

Luis looked at her in surprise. "Seven points? For one goal? That's different, too," he said. "In soccer, a goal is just one point."

Mary nodded her head in agreement. "Yes, but American football is scored differently, too," she explained. "If the team gets the ball over the goal line, that's a touchdown for six points. After that, they get a kick. If the ball goes through the goal posts, they get an extra point. If the ball doesn't go through, there's no extra point."

"I see," Luis laughed. "I've never even scored five points in a football game back home, so that's a lot of points for me!"

EXTRA!

MAIN WAYS TO SCORE IN AMERICAN FOOTBALL

Touchdown (6 points): a team carries or throws the ball and catches it over the goal line

Extra Point (1 point): a team kicks the ball through the goal posts after a touchdown

Extra Point (2 points): a team carries or throws the ball and catches it over the goal line after a touchdown

Field Goal (3 points): a team kicks the ball through the goal posts with no touchdown

official

stripes

Luis made Mary giggle by comparing zebras and officials. He made her laugh a little.

After the touchdown, Luis noticed some people had come on the field. He gave Mary a strange look. The people were wearing black and white striped shirts. "Who are those guys?" he asked.

"Oh, they're the **officials**," explained Mary. "They make sure everyone follows the game rules."

"Got it," replied Luis. "But they remind me of something. . . ." Luis thought for a while. In soccer, the officials wear colored shirts and black shorts. The American officials looked really different and looked like something else to him, but he couldn't think of it. Suddenly, he turned to Mary and said excitedly, "I got it! They kind of remind me of zebras!"

Mary bent over laughing. "You're so funny, Luis!" she giggled. "I'm really glad you came!"

American
Football

About   Championships   Videos   Gallery

Football Officials

There are usually seven football officials in an American football game. They watch the game and players carefully to make sure everyone follows the rules. If a player or team doesn't follow the rules, the officials stop the game. Every time they stop the game, the clock stops. A football game is supposed to last 90 minutes, but the average game is over two hours long! That shows you how often the officials have to step in!

After a few more minutes, the game was over. There were no more touchdowns, so the red team won with their single score! Luis and Mary and the other fans were really happy, and the players were even happier!

"Thanks for explaining things to me, Mary," said Luis as the fans were **cheering** around them. "American football is an exciting game. I really like it."

"Yes, it's one of my favorite sports," replied Mary over the crowd.

As he looked around the stadium at all the people, Luis turned to Mary and said, "You know what Mary? American football and soccer are not that different after all."

"Oh really? What do you mean?" asked Mary.

"Well, the rules are different. And the players are different. But the most important thing is not different. Winning is always fun for everyone!" explained Luis with a smile and a cheer.

"That's right, Luis," replied Mary laughing. "That's very very right!"

Main Differences between American Football and Soccer

	American football	Soccer
Color of ball	brown	black and white
What they wear	helmet, shoulder pads, jersey, cleats	shorts, T-shirts
Number of officials	up to 7	3–4
How they move the ball	throw, carry, kick	kick
Point system	up to 7 points a touchdown	1 point a goal

stadium a special building or place for sporting events

field the area on which you play a sport

player a person who is taking part in a game

helmet protective head cover worn by athletes

uniform special clothing that is worn by all people playing or doing something together

confidence a feeling of sureness, certainty

confusion a feeling of not understanding

defensive trying to prevent another person or team from scoring in a game

offensive trying to score points in a game

goal post / goal line the two upright posts and line that players cross to score in American football

touchdown a six-point score made by carrying the ball into the end zone

official a person who controls a game or sporting event because he or she knows the rules well

cheer to shout or call out to support a team or person